Whispers Aloud

POETiC WORDS OF ART

BOOK ONE

BY GEE SIDNEY PITTMAN

Welcome

(BIENVENIDO)

DEDICATION

I AM THE TORCH THAT YOU WILL CARRY

I am the torch that you will carry
Every minute of every hour,
I am the torch that you will carry
Your indomitable source of power.

I am the torch that you will carry
While sweat-drenched in sun,
I am the torch that you will carry
When the day seems never done.

I am the torch that you will carry
When the nights get a little colder,
I am the torch that you will carry
While looking over your shoulder.

I am the torch that you will carry
When you have not slept,
I am the torch that you will carry
On every mission you accept.

I am the torch that you will carry
I will never leave you alone,
I am the torch that you will carry
And, I will **Carry You** safely-**Home**.

· Amen ·

Whispers Aloud

ORDER OF CONTENT

Exordium

SOL

"There is a standard in which,
I have created to which, I am immured."

Whispers Aloud

CHAPTER I

PERSONAL AND CONFIDENTIAL

DEAREST ONE

Dearest One,

How are you doing? Fine, I hope and well. Oh, I have a little 'something' for you I have to tell. While it's been some time now since we've seen each other last, what I have to say - believe me - is not an easy task. It is about the night we spent together Dearest, eleven months ago, and how we both submitted to ardent passion, ever consensually so.   How we acceded to coitus, and being prudent and cautious, while not knowing then, such a heavy price it would cost us. You must have some idea I know, just 'read between the lines.' Ready or not, Dearest One, I gave birth to 'one of your kind.'

But rest assured 'must' will be done. I feel no damn shame. But things would make to be much easier if I did know your name. In closing this letter, I would like to say, "take heed to what I mean: he is 'truly yours,' Dearest One…

Sincerely,
Billy Jean

P.S.
So hard to forget those climaxing moments, singed with enraptured joy.
So easy to remember the smiling face of our brand-new baby boy.

I, COLORED MAN

Standing in front of a full-length mirror
For the naked eye to see,
Is an empirical continuum of time and space
I, Colored Man is me.

If you like what you see
Do something to love it,
If you don't like what you see
Do something to rise above it-
Forthwith.

There are people, places and omnifarious things
That will make or break you in stride,
So, be ready, be willing, but never succumb
To the phrase, "At least I tried."

Oh, be able this man,
Who did not know his father.
Be able this man,
He just didn't care to bother.
Be able this man,
It can be a lonely place.
Be able this man,
'Suit up' and run this race.

And while you are running,
I want you to remember these words.
Words of truth that are free of surmise,
Replete with sagacity, not meant to disguise:

"Without a beautiful and talented superior woman
in your life, you are sure to be beaten and bruised by
strife."

The End

'LIGHT YOUR WAY AGAIN'

I know sometimes, the road seems long
And there seems no end in sight,
So you throw in the towel because you are all 'fought out'
Declaring the end of the fight.

§

I know sometimes, through sweat and strain
It isn't clear to see what lies ahead,
And if a choice was given, you would be livin'
The worth of **you** instead.

§

I know sometimes that a tear may fall
More often than not, and when it does,
How you wish to befriend a thing called, 'happy'
To be where sadness was.

§

I know sometimes, it is hard to be strong
But you know, the strongest survive,
And it's at that moment, you cherish the thought
Of how good it is to be alive.

§

Sometimes I know, and He knows it too
That nightfall brings a little rain,
Just look to Him in your darkest hour
And, He will 'Light Your Way Again.'

· Amen·

I OFTEN WONDER

I often wonder
What the world would be like,
If it had no streams
Or mountains to hike.
If it had no clouds
To bring us rain,
Or heartache from heartbreak
Steeped in pain.
If it had no sun
The 'Guiding Light,'
Or the falling of day
Into the arms of night.
If it had no wars
For which to declare,
Or the high cost of living
That seems not quite fair.
If it had no schools
Or A, B, C's,
Or the science to cure
The most virulent disease.
If it had no laws
No liberties,
No 'tis of thee'

Or to 'thee I sing.'
But what if the world said,
"Here, take me, I'm yours."
I would open all the windows
Leave ajar all the doors.
All that was lost
Would now be found,
Turn the most odious frown
Upside down.
Extirpate darkness
Illuminate light,
All that was wrong
Would have a chance to make it right.
No person versus pigment
No language preferred,
'Power' is with the people
I give you my word.
But what would the world be like?
You know, 'I Often Wonder.'

The End

SAN

To the committee, to the chairperson, to the institution,
  I am grateful to all of you, for honoring me with this
  prestigious award.

§

In furtherance, there are those that I need to give 'thank
  you' to in my entirety.

§

I 'thank you' to my Lord and Savior for all of His
    omnipotence and for the relationship we have that
allows my existence.
I 'thank you' to the enslaved of yesterday, and the
    enslaved of today.
And to their tired, worn and compromised feet, traveling
    on dirt roads and concrete that paved a way.
I 'thank you' to the families of King, Jackson and Davis,
And to Pops and their family led by his daughter Mavis.
I 'thank you' to Robeson, Poitier, Lena and Billie of jazz
    and blues.
And, to all of my 'babies' who love their 'Pappa,' I 'thank
    you' and love all of you, too.

§

In cessation, I woud like to leave a few words with you this morning.

Words of veracity, that will also, include, epithetical derision that I will extrude.

§

To all of those Caucasian and non-Caucasian eyes looking at me, looking at you. I want you to know that I know-what you are thinking and saying- and keeping on the 'Down Low:'

§

"Gosh man, that Gee Sidney Pittman, head just got a little bigga. Don't freak, because when it's all said and done, he is still a Nigga."

§

To you all (Hand love 'signs' over heart).
And may God Bless You – Everyone.

·The End·

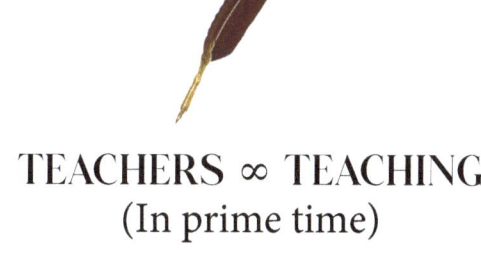

TEACHERS ∞ TEACHING
(In prime time)

This is needed. Please read it.
Every line and space,
It ain't sugar and spice, and everything's nice
It is acrid, and bitter to taste.

§

Don't just listen to our needs and cries
Of a learned education,
And don't try to assuage, you do need to
gauge, the temperature of our frustration.

§

Every day in every way
We push against a pull,
We catechize, we compromise
Although our plates are full.

§

The faux walls that obscure, not assure
The A B C's of life,
While we all limp to the finish line
Overwhelmed with strife.

From top to bottom, inside and out
Rebuild, sans brick and stone,
And, the A E I's, O's and U's,
Will be blessings to have known.

§

Extra! Extra! Read all about it
We 'now' have just been heard,
No doubt about it. Let's shout about it
Every written word.

· The End ·

THANKSGIVING DAY

Bless**ed** is the homemaker
Polishing chrome,
Wretch**ed** is the cardboard
He calls his home.

Bless**ed** is the table
Of plenary treats,
Wretch**ed** is the food line
Twenty people deep.

So, when blessing your table
On this day of giving,
Think about others
And how they are living.

Needed communion and prayer
Is sure to find their way,
With answers they have sought

On **Thanksgiving Day**.

· Amen ·

TRIUMPH

I choose to look up
Instead of looking down,
Attired in elation
Instead of a naked frown.

§

There are those who have tried
To taint me with pain,
Embitter my spirit
Curse me in name.

§

But, I will not waver
Nor shall I endure,
Another's caustic woefulness
That, I can assure.

§

And with God as my Witness
I am encouraged to say,
'If there is a mountain to climb
I will do it, my way.' **TRIUMPH!**

· Amen ·

YOU GOTTA LOOK GOOD WHILE YOU'RE DOING IT

Whether you are mixing matter to create compost
Or 'compliments of the Rosa's' caterer and host-
'You Gotta Look Good While You're Doing It.'

Whether raking a yard or sweeping a street
Or the 'back-seat driver' in the passenger's seat-
'You Gotta Look Good While You're Doing It.'

Whether a storm has rendered you
    enervated and without power,
Or getting an 'emergency' call in the midnight hour-
'You Gotta Look Good While You're Doing It.'

Whether you hold 'em or fold 'em,
    hedging or placing a bet,
Promising the world ain't seen the best of you yet-
'You Gotta Look Good While You're Doing It.'

Twenty-four hours each and every day
For all of God's blessings you bow and say,
"Thank you, Father," and 'Look Good While You're Doing It.'

· The End ·

23

Whispers Aloud

CHAPTER II

Isms, Idioms & Aphorisms

· (State of Mind) ·

Your 'State of mind' is only as healthy
as the food you use for thought

§

Fritter

If you 're not organized, you can't capitalize

§

· (I.D.) ·

The way you represent yourself is the way you
will be identified.

§

· (P.R.) ·

Proof is in the results.

§

· (Penny of Cents) ·

A penny makes it all make cents.

Mindful

Mind your own business, and only to you let it be known. Because once rumor makes news of it, it is no longer your own.

Shoes of Credibility

Money can take you a lot of places, but credibility are the shoes to be worn to get you there, so one should never leave home without them. . . One should never leave home without the 'shoes of credibility,' to be worn to get you where money can take you.

§

I'm Afraid...Not

Remember:
No matter how hard the task
Or how scared the tear,
Hastened courage
Foils the fright in fear.

Vie

In your pursuit to succeed
Effort cannot be neglected,
While mistakes and errors are made
Failure is never accepted.

Whispers Aloud

EPILOGUE

REFLECTiONS

(IN MEMORIA)

She wore a 'fine brown frame'
Standing five feet tall,
Hair-bouncing on her waistline
Wait. That is not all.

§

'Woman of the Hour' in the kitchen
Food flourishing with taste,
Whether slicin' or dicin'
Not a thing went to waste.

§

Oh, how she loved her sports
And to see her watching games,
Be it courtside or ringside
She knew 'skill levels' and names.

§

What joy of a mother
What a joy of a friend,
The first - 'girl of my dreams'
That suddenly, came to an end.

§

I miss more than a mother
Artificer, matriarch and wife,
I miss that 'Woman of the Hour'
Every day of my life. . .I love you, Mama.

· Amen ·

ABOUT THE AUTHOR

Gee Sidney Pittman:

Was born, reared, and nurtured in the Southern (South) area of the USA. Early in his childhood, Gee became aware of his philous for vocabulary, music, and dance which is an abridged list of what Gee endeared himself to. On television, inchoative at the age of six years old, he was enamored of performing artists. From Mitzi Gaynor to Fred Astaire; from Ginger Rogers to James Cagney; and from Sammy Davis, Jr. to Michael Jackson. He loved them all. He said, "These are legitimate, legendary performers with artistic prowess who showcased their multifarious talents on stage and screen; and to whom I began being an audience to at the age of six years old. The common thread woven through the pockets of their abilities, thereby monogramming the omphalos of their identities, was dance. And I have been blessed with the opportunity and privilege to have been able to bare witness thereto."

Shirley A. Dozier

Thank You

(GRACIAS)

www.ingramcontent.com/pod-product-compliance
Lightning Source LLC
Chambersburg PA
CBHW040905120626
46551CB00006B/657